Lewis and Clark

Lewis and Clark

Andrew Santella

Watts LIBRARY

Franklin Watts
A Division of Scholastic Inc.
New York • Toronto • London • Auckland • Sydney
Mexico City • New Delhi • Hong Kong
Danbury, Connecticut

Note to readers: Definitions for words in **bold** can be found in the Glossary at the back of this book.

Map by XNR Productions

The illustration on the cover shows Meriwether Lewis and William Clark. The photograph opposite the title page shows the Missouri River.

Cover illustration by Stephen Marchesi.

Photographs ©: American Philosophical Society Library, Philadelphia: 40, 43; Christie's Images: 8; Corbis-Bettmann: 5, 20 (Scott T. Smith), 34; Culver Pictures: 31; National Museum of American History, Smithsonian Institution: 17; Collection of the New-York Historical Society: 12; North Wind Picture Archives: 5, 9, 11, 14, 16, 23, 24, 26, 28, 30, 32, 47, 52, 53; Photo Researchers, NY/Jeff Lepore: 48; St. Louis Mercantile Library at the University of Missouri, St. Louis: 50; Stock Montage, Inc.: 42, 45 (Newberry Library), 35, 37; Stone/Jake Rajs: 6, 7; Superstock, Inc.: 51 (David David Gallery, Philadelphia), 38, 39; Unicorn Stock Photos/Aneal S. Vohra: 2.

Library of Congress Cataloging-in-Publication Data

Santella, Andrew
    Lewis and Clark / by Andrew Santella
        p. cm.— (Watts Library)
    Includes bibliographical references (p.) and index.
    ISBN 0-531-20323-9 (lib. bdg.)   0-531-16581-7 (pbk.)
    1. Lewis and Clark Expedition (1804–1806)—Juvenile literature. 2. West (U.S.)—Discovery and exploration—Juvenile literature. 3. Lewis, Meriwether, 1774–1809—Juvenile literature. 4. Clark, William, 1770–1838—Juvenile literature. [1. Lewis and Clark Expedition (1804–1806). 2. West (U.S.)—Discovery and exploration. 3. Lewis, Meriwether, 1774–1809. 4. Clark, William, 1770–1838. 5. Explorers.] I. Title. II. Series.
F592.7 .S1244   2001
917.804′2—dc21
                                                                  00-046251

Contents

In 1800, Americans knew very little about the West.

Chapter One

The Mysterious West

In 1800, the lands of the American West were a great mystery to most Americans. They knew the land beyond the Mississippi River was rich with valuable resources, such as animal furs. They also knew the land stretched for thousands of miles to the Pacific Ocean. Beyond that, they could only guess.

Some people believed that prehistoric

Man of the People

Thomas Jefferson became the third president of the United States in 1801 and held office for two terms, retiring in 1809. Before becoming president, Jefferson wrote the Declaration of Independence.

animals like the **woolly mammoth** were still walking the Great Plains. Others said you could find a mountain of pure salt somewhere in the West. The president of the United States—Thomas Jefferson—wondered about reports of an American Indian tribe out west that spoke Welsh.

When it came to the American West, no one really knew what to believe. When Jefferson was elected president in 1800, the land west of the Mississippi River didn't even belong to the United States. The area between the Mississippi and the Pacific Ocean was largely up for grabs. Spain, France, Great Britain, Russia, and the United States all made claims to various parts of it—and nations of American Indians already lived there.

Most Americans lived in a narrow **swath** of land along the Atlantic Ocean. Some adventurous settlers had already moved into the region that is now Ohio, Indiana, Illinois, Kentucky, and Tennessee. Beyond that area, thousands of miles of uncharted territory stretched to the Pacific Ocean.

President Jefferson wanted to know more about this land and the American Indians who lived on it. He hoped to learn what sorts of plants and animals could be found there, and what valuable minerals. Three times Jefferson tried to organize expeditions to the West to find out. Finally, when he became president, Jefferson did send a group west to learn more. They would be the first to attempt such a trip. Their assignment was to travel up the Missouri River to its source in the Rocky Mountains. Then they would have to find a path across the unexplored mountains. Finally, they would follow the Columbia River to the Pacific Ocean. Their goal was to find a water route across America.

The men who would lead the expedition were no strangers to Jefferson. Both were from his home state of Virginia. One was Jefferson's personal **secretary**. His name was Meriwether Lewis.

Meriwether Lewis

Meriwether Lewis

Meriwether Lewis was born in Albermarle County, Virginia, on August 18, 1774. He hardly knew his father, because Lieutenant William Lewis was fighting the Revolutionary War during much of his son's early life. In 1779, the lieutenant died of **pneumonia**, leaving Meriwether, his sister Jane, and his brother Reuben fatherless.

His mother, Lucy, married another army officer, Captain John Marks, in 1780. Captain Marks introduced young Meriwether to the

Lewis's Mom

Lucy Meriwether Lewis Marks lived to be eighty-six years old. Lewis remained close to his mother throughout his life. He even wrote to her while he was exploring the West.

wilderness. When he was just eight years old, Meriwether went with his stepfather to Georgia to help establish a new settlement there. It was his first trip through wild, unsettled country.

As much as he learned from his stepfather, Meriwether learned more from his mother. She passed along to Meriwether her knowledge of the natural world. She taught him about the properties and characteristics of the trees and shrubs around them. She quizzed her son on the names of the birds and insects they encountered. His familiarity with the natural world served him well later on his great adventure.

When Lewis turned twenty-one, he joined the United States Army, with the rank of ensign. Within a year, he was assigned to an elite company of riflemen. His captain was also from Virginia—a man named William Clark. In the six months the two men served together, they grew to respect each other greatly. From this friendship grew one of the great partnerships of American history.

William Clark

Born on August 1, 1770, in Caroline County, Virginia, William Clark was the youngest of six sons and the ninth child in a family of ten. His older brother, George Rogers Clark, was one of the best-known heroes of the Revolutionary War. William, too young to fight, must have itched for his own chance at glory. He was just fourteen when he moved west with the rest of his family to settle near Louisville, Kentucky, in 1784.

Young red-haired William developed a special bond with his famous older brother. From George Clark, he learned about soldiering, survival in the wilderness, and the ways of American Indians. He couldn't have picked a better instructor in the wilderness skills that would serve him well on his own trip to the Pacific Ocean two decades later. By the time he was nineteen, William joined the Kentucky **militia**.

William Clark

In 1791, he joined the U.S. Army. He served for five years, fighting American Indians in Ohio and Indiana. His bravery and leadership skills won him the attention of his commanding officers. Clark was given command of an elite rifle company at Fort Greenville, Ohio, in 1795. When Meriwether Lewis was assigned to his company, the two hit it off immediately. They were both from well-known Virginia families and had extensive wilderness experience. Each had served in the militia as well as in the regular army. They both stood about 6 feet (183 centimeters) tall. But they were also different from each other in important ways. Lewis was quieter, more thoughtful, and moody while Clark was outgoing and even-tempered. Lewis was better educated while Clark had been raised to be a man of action. They complemented each other perfectly, each having the qualities the other lacked. It's no wonder that their names are forever linked.

Meriwether Lewis did all that he could to prepare for the expedition.

Chapter Two

The Corps of Discovery

President Jefferson asked Lewis to lead the expedition to explore the American West. Then he made sure that Lewis received the best education possible to prepare him for the trip. Jefferson sent Lewis on a tour to meet America's most learned men. Lewis met with Andrew Ellicot, the nation's leading astronomer and mathematician. He also worked with map collector Albert Gallatin. He consulted with the eminent physician Dr. Benjamin Rush. And he took lessons in

botany from Dr. Benjamin Smith Barton. He also collected books on science and geography to take West.

Jefferson expected a lot from the expedition he organized. He called the group the Corps of Discovery—and he wanted the explorers to be prepared to make discoveries of all kinds. They were instructed to carefully observe and learn from the American Indians they met along the way. They were ordered to note and record the plant and animal life and the mineral resources they encountered. They would have to learn to use the sun and the moon to chart the course of their travels.

When Lewis finished his crash course, he called on his old friend. In June of 1803, he wrote to William Clark, offering him the co-command of the expedition. Lewis told Clark, "there is no man on earth with whom I should feel equal plea-

This photograph shows Lewis's invitation to Clark to share command of the expedition.

sure in sharing [the honor of command] as with yourself." Clark accepted.

Jefferson wrote instructions for Lewis. The aim of the trip would be to explore the Missouri River to find "the most direct and practicable [practical] water communication across the continent for purposes of commerce." Jefferson gave special instructions regarding relations with American Indians. He told Lewis that he should "treat them in the most friendly . . . manner which their own conduct will admit."

An Empty Map

Lewis and Clark had no road map for their trip. The best maps of the time showed only huge blank spaces in the West. Certainly, fur trappers had begun using the Missouri River, but they had ventured only about as far as modern-day North Dakota. On the Pacific coast, merchant ships started trading with American Indians and even made their way inland on large rivers, such as the Columbia. But in between were vast and unknown regions. This was the land that Jefferson wanted to know about.

Some people thought the Missouri River might offer a way to travel to the Pacific Ocean.

Jefferson hoped Lewis and Clark would find a dependable water route between the Pacific Ocean and the Great Plains. Everyone knew the Missouri River started somewhere in the mountains of the West and headed east. Everyone knew the Columbia River also started somewhere in the mountains, and headed in the opposite direction. Everyone hoped that the two rivers started very near each other. If only a day or so of land travel separated the two rivers, traders in boats could make their way back and forth with ease. It would mean a boom in commerce for whoever controlled the West.

Getting Ready

Lewis spent months getting ready for the trip. He selected the best new **compasses** and other navigating and map-making devices. He invented a watertight container made of lead to hold gunpowder. And he designed a new rifle for the journey. He gathered the best medicines available at that time. He

This photograph shows the compass used by Lewis during the expedition.

Price of Discovery

Congress set aside $2,500 to pay for the Lewis and Clark expedition. The trip ended up costing $39,000.

packed flannel shirts, blankets, and backpacks. He also got presents for the American Indians he would meet: mirrors, tobacco, brass kettles, and 4,600 sewing needles.

Lewis also oversaw the building of a **keelboat**. A keelboat was the preferred craft for rivers in the early 1800s. Lewis's keelboat was 55 feet (17 meters) long and 8 feet (2 m) wide in the middle. It had a 32-foot (10-m) tall mast that could support a square sail. But that would be useful only when the wind was at their backs. Otherwise, the boat would move by muscle power. On deck were eleven benches for the oarsmen. It took weeks to build the keelboat.

The expedition would use smaller boats too. Lewis planned to take the keelboat only part-way up the river. The explorers traveled some of the way in **pirogues**—large flat-bottomed rowboats. Traveling up the Missouri, they would make their own canoes. They hacked them out of the trunks of cottonwood trees.

Lewis set off down the Ohio River from Pittsburgh on August 31, 1803. Two months later, he joined up with Clark in Indiana. Along the way, Lewis and Clark recruited twenty-seven members for their expedition, including some soldiers

The Air Gun

Lewis used his own money to buy a rifle he hoped would impress American Indians he would meet on the trip. It worked like a BB gun, firing bullets by compressed air—no need for gunpowder or flints. Lewis gave many demonstrations of the rifle.

In Sickness and Health

Lewis and Clark thought of nearly everything they would need for their trip—except a doctor. When one of their men became ill or injured, Lewis and Clark tried to treat him themselves. Neither Lewis nor Clark had formal training as a doctor. But not many people in America did. The first medical school in America wasn't founded until 1768, just a few decades before the expedition. Dr. Benjamin Rush had given Lewis a list of "health rules." He told Lewis to have the men wear flannel, especially in winter. The commanders followed that suggestion. Rush also told him to let the men lie down when they grew tired. The commanders probably didn't always follow that rule.

from army posts, woodsmen, and farmers. Anyone who wasn't already a soldier was then enlisted in the U.S. Army. Lewis and Clark also signed on a trapper and hunter named George Drouillard who knew Indian sign languages. And Clark also brought along his slave, York, to serve as cook and assistant to the leaders.

The group set up winter camp in Illinois, near where the Missouri River flows into the Mississippi. For the next three years, this group would depend on one another for their survival. They would see sights and encounter people that no American had ever known. And they would overcome obstacles that they couldn't yet even imagine.

The waters of the Missouri River proved to be treacherous for Lewis and Clark.

Chapter Three

Up the Missouri

The Missouri River in springtime rushes east, fed by melting mountain snow. Sometimes the current carries with it whole trees ripped from the riverbank. In the spring of 1804, Lewis and Clark headed west up the Missouri—against that strong current. On May 14, the party set off from its winter camp but they made just 4 miles (6 km) before they had to stop. It was the first sign of the hardships and obstacles that lay ahead.

The expedition soon settled into a routine. On good days, the party traveled about 20 miles (32 km) on the water. Hunting parties went out on horseback each morning and returned to the boats by nightfall. At night, the group tried to camp on islands in the river, for security. One of the men, Pierre Cruzatte, had brought his fiddle and he played for the party after they finished eating. Most of the time, Clark stayed on the keelboat, where his river skills came in handy, while Lewis walked on shore.

Life on the river was **grueling**. It may have been the easiest way to travel west in those days, but it was still very difficult. The party was heading upstream, working against a current of about 5 miles (8 km) per hour that was pushing them in the opposite direction. When the winds were favorable, the party could raise their sails and glide along with the wind. However, most of the time, the explorers had to use their muscles to move the boats. They used oars to paddle the crafts forward or pulled the boats from shore with towropes. The men struggled through knee-deep water and mud, hauling the boats behind them. The summer heat and clouds of mosquitoes did not make the job easier. The river was full of hazards too. Jagged trunks of dead trees lay underneath the surface of the water, waiting to rip a hole in the bottom of a boat.

Natural Wonders

As he walked along the riverbank, Lewis noticed the plants and animals of the West. He saw that **game** was plentiful and admired the beautiful landscape. "Immense herds of buffalo, deer, elk and antelopes we saw every day," Lewis wrote in his journal. Clark was also impressed. He wrote, using his irregular spelling, "what a field for a botents [botanist] and a natirless [**naturalist**]."

Lewis and Clark saw buffalo, pelicans, and coyotes, all of which were new to them. Jefferson had sent the explorers west partly to record the natural world there. Since the camera had not been invented yet, Lewis and Clark had to use paper and pencil to describe and show what they saw. They both kept journals and ordered their sergeants to do so too. They filled those journals with descriptions and sketches of the new

This photograph shows the journal Clark kept during the expedition.

plants, animals, and landscapes. Sometimes they collected samples of the **flora** and **fauna** to send back to Jefferson.

Meeting the Teton Sioux

By August, they were in what was known as **Indian country** at the time. Their first meeting with a party of Oto and Missouri Indians went well. The soldiers paraded and Lewis

Lewis and Clark tried to make friends with each Indian group they encountered.

Eating on the Trail

The members of Lewis and Clark's expedition couldn't be picky eaters. They started out eating army rations like salt pork. Soon, they were eating corn, beans, and squash they got from Indians. They also tried dog meat, horse-meat, and even beaver tail. In the barren mountains, they survived by eating roots. On the plentiful plains each member ate as much as 9 pounds (4 kilograms) of bison meat every day. That's equal to thirty-six hamburgers.

and Clark gave the Indians flags, medals, and whisky. To impress the Indians, they demonstrated how a compass worked. A meeting several weeks later with a band of Yankton Sioux was also peaceful. But further upriver waited the Teton Sioux.

The expedition party knew the Teton Sioux Indians had been threatening trappers who had pushed upriver from St. Louis. Lewis and Clark first met the Teton Sioux near present-day Pierre, South Dakota. The expedition's leaders met with the tribe's chiefs on board the keelboat. During this meeting, one of the chiefs—Partisan—became angry. He shoved Clark and demanded more gifts. Clark tried to get Partisan off the boat. That only made the chief angrier. His warriors grabbed the boat's towline and refused to let the party continue upriver. Clark, on the riverbank, drew his sword. Lewis, on board the keelboat, ordered his men to ready their rifles. Both sides prepared for a fight, but the Sioux backed off. Then a chief named Black Buffalo ordered that the towline be released and the expedition was able to continue.

The Corps of Discovery's only **casualty** was not the result of conflicts with Indians, however. Sergeant Charles Floyd died of what Lewis called "biliose chorlick." Most likely, he suffered from a burst appendix. Floyd was the first U.S. soldier to die west of the Mississippi River. Lewis and Clark buried him with military honors.

Winter Quarters

By the end of October, the party had arrived at the villages of the Mandan and Hidatsa Indians, about 60 miles (97 km) upriver from present-day Bismarck, North Dakota. The

This illustration shows what a Mandan village looked like in the 1800s.

Little "Pomp"

Sacagawea's son, Jean Baptiste, was born on February 13, 1805. Clark gave him the nickname "Pomp," perhaps inspired by a fiddle tune of that name. His likeness appears on the $1 coin. He can be seen strapped to his mother's back—just the way he traveled to the Pacific Ocean and back.

Mandans were farmers and hunters who lived in round, domed houses. About four thousand Mandans lived in these villages, more people than lived in Washington, D.C., at that time. The party's relations with the Mandans were mostly peaceful. The Indians were especially intrigued by York, the first black man they had ever seen.

Lewis and Clark built a fort near the villages to serve as their winter camp. It was an icy and bitter cold winter. Temperatures dropped as low as –45 degrees Fahrenheit (–43 degrees Celsius) and the Missouri River froze solid. Fortunately, Fort Mandan was ready by Christmas. The party spent the long winter making repairs and preparing for their departure in the spring. They also added two more people to their group. They signed on a trapper named Toussaint Charbonneau to act as an interpreter. He brought with him his Shoshone wife, Sacagawea, who was pregnant. In the rough days ahead, Sacagawea would serve the expedition well.

27

Along with the samples they collected, Lewis and Clark included information from their journals in their report to President Jefferson.

Chapter Four

Into the Unknown

By the winter of 1805, Lewis and Clark had already made many new discoveries. They had spotted and captured their first prairie dog—it took nearly a full day to catch the animal. They had gathered and sketched plants that were new to them. Lewis and Clark spent much of the winter at Fort Mandan preparing a report to Jefferson about what they found so far. It was their homework and it was due before they headed farther west in the spring. They put their notes, their maps,

their sketches, and even the prairie dog in a package and sent it to Jefferson.

Lewis and Clark gave their report to a group of soldiers who would return home early on the big keelboat. Three months passed before the report reached President Jefferson in Washington. At that time, communications traveled only as quickly as boats and horses would allow.

A New Frontier

The Corps of Discovery continued west from Fort Mandan on April 7, 1805, with thirty-three people traveling on the Missouri River in six canoes and two pirogues. Now they were heading into the unknown. For more than a year, there would be no communication with the world back east. They were going places no American had ever been and the new discoveries came in bunches. They saw their first moose, first

Members of the expedition fire on the grizzly.

Seaman

Lewis brought a dog along on the trip. He was a big, black Newfoundland dog named Seaman and he did his share of the work. He chased down squirrels that provided dinner for the hungry explorers. At night, his barking warned the men of approaching grizzlies. When a Shawnee chief tried to trade three beaver skins for Seaman, Lewis angrily turned him down.

bighorn sheep, and first grizzly bear. American Indians in the area hunted the grizzly in groups of at least ten men because they so respected the animals' power. Lewis and Clark's men had to learn this lesson the hard way. In mid-May, a group of six hunters sneaked up on a 500-pound (227-kg) grizzly and opened fire. Four shots hit the bear, but the animal was barely wounded. Enraged, the bear charged the hunters. The animal chased four of the men a long distance to the river and almost managed to swim to one of them, before it was finally killed by a shot from the riverbank. When the men examined the bear, they found eight bullets in its body. Lewis had seen enough of the fearsome creature. He wrote, "I find that the curiosity of our party is pretty well satisfied with rispect [respect] to this animal."

As they continued on the Missouri, the explorers came to a part of the river that was flanked by 300-foot (91-m) high **bluffs**. The bluffs were sculpted by wind, rain, and snow into wonderful shapes. Farther down the river, the explorers faced their greatest test yet. In June, they came to the Great Falls

The Great Falls of the Missouri River presented a great obstacle to the expedition.

The *Experiment*

Lewis brought a portable boat with him. Its frame was iron, but it was light and it could be covered with animal skins and used to carry four tons of supplies. Such a boat had never been tested before, so Lewis called it the *Experiment*. The *Experiment* failed. Its seams leaked and the boat took on too much water. Lewis buried it and ordered more canoes made instead.

of the Missouri River. They had heard the roar of the waterfall 7 miles (11 km) away. Lewis, the first to see the falls, called them "the greatest sight I ever beheld." Describing one of the falls, he wrote, "[T]he river pitches over a shelving rock, with an edge as regular and streight as if formed by art, without a niche or brake in it; the water decends in one even and uninterupted sheet to the bottom wher dashing against the rocky bottom [it] rises into foaming billows of great height and rappidly glides away, hising flashing and sparkling as it departs . . . I now thought that if a skillfull painter had been asked to make a beautiful cascade that he would most probably have p[r]esented the precise immage of this one."

They may have been beautiful, but the falls meant trouble for the explorers. Since their boats could not go over the falls, the group had to **portage** around them. They had been traveling 18 miles (29 km) a day on the river. Now it would take them almost four weeks to travel the same distance overland. They made crude wagons to carry their supplies across **ravines** and up steep slopes. They were hampered every step of the way by sharp **prickly pear** thorns and jagged rocks.

Sacagawea helped the expedition find her people, the Shoshone.

Searching for the Shoshone

As they neared the Rocky Mountains, Lewis and Clark began watching for signs of the Shoshone Indians. The Shoshone were known for their herds of horses, which would be needed for crossing the mountains. Sacagawea was a Shoshone Indian but she hadn't seen her people or her home since she was captured years before by a neighboring tribe. Soon, however, she began to recognize her people's familiar landmarks.

On August 13, Lewis and a small group finally came upon three Shoshone women digging for roots. Warned of the approach of the party, sixty warriors rode out from their village

34

Sacagawea

Sacagawea was just a teenager when she traveled with Lewis and Clark. She endured all the hardships the men endured—and she was also caring for her baby Jean Baptiste. Sacagawea means "bird woman" in the Shoshone language. As an interpreter, Sacagawea played an important part in acquiring horses from the Shoshone. She also saved important equipment and journals during a river accident. Lewis and Clark named a river after her. Today, her likeness is on the $1 coin. She died in 1812. Clark raised Sacagawea's son Jean Baptiste and her daughter, Lisette.

to meet them. Lewis convinced the warriors that his expedition came in peace. Four days later, Clark and the rest of the party arrived. Sacagawea was brought forward to serve as an interpreter for talks with Chief Cameahwait. Before long, she realized that Chief Cameahwait was her brother. The two had not seen each other in many years. Amid tears of joy, she told

Lewis and Clark that her people would provide horses and guides to lead them across the mountains. It would be the most difficult part of the journey yet.

For a week, Lewis, Clark, and the rest of the expedition had seen the snow-capped Bitterroot Range in the distance. Sergeant Patrick Gass called them "the most terrible mountains I ever beheld." Lewis and Clark knew from the Shoshone that their trail would take them over some of the roughest terrain in the Rockies.

Help From the Nez Percé

By August 26, temperatures had fallen to the freezing mark. Fallen timber blocked their trail. The party scrambled up steep slopes and down deep gorges. When they reached a high vantage point, they could see nothing but more snow-covered mountains in every direction. Food supplies dwindled. Game was so scarce that the men killed and roasted one of their horses. On September 16, it began snowing early in the morning and continued all day. The leaders decided that the only

Friend or Foe

Lewis and Clark were determined to build good relations with the American Indians they met. They weren't always successful, though. They exchanged threats with the Teton Sioux and shot it out with a group of Blackfeet. But Lewis and Clark did make some friends among the Indians. In their first cold winter on the plains, the Mandans gave them corn to eat. And the Nez Percé helped them when the explorers were at their weakest.

way they would make it through alive was for Clark to push ahead with a small party. They hoped to find the Nez Percé Indians and trade for food.

Within a few days, Clark came to a Nez Percé village. Lewis and the rest of the party arrived a few days later. The Nez Percé supplied the hungry explorers with salmon, berries, and roots. They had survived starvation, cold, and extreme fatigue. But now many of them became violently ill from the unfamiliar diet of the Nez Percé.

Lying exhausted and ill at the Nez Percé village, the members of the expedition were virtually helpless. The tribe could have easily wiped them out. The Nez Percé could have taken all the party's supplies and guns, and become one of the richest tribes in the West. But the Nez Percé did not turn on the explorers. Instead, they agreed to help the party build boats for the next

Lewis and the rest of the expedition struggled through the Rockies.

leg of the expedition. Clearly grateful, the journals of Lewis and Clark are filled with expressions of admiration for the Nez Percé culture.

To the Pacific

The expedition had made it across the mountains—but it had taken weeks. Their hope for an easy water route between the Pacific and North America was crushed. But there was still more to learn. In early October, the expedition was on water again. Now they were traveling downstream, with the river's current pushing them toward their destination. They traveled first on the Clearwater River, then on the Snake, and finally on the mighty Columbia. This was the river that would take them at last to the Pacific Ocean. Signs of the distant ocean were already everywhere. The Indians they met carried copper kettles and wore sailors' jackets. This meant they had traded with coastal Indians. Lewis and Clark were moving ever nearer their goal. First, though, they had to run a 55-mile (88-km) stretch of rough waters on the Columbia. The river has a series of dangerous rapids and falls as it cuts through the Cascade Mountains. The Nez Percé on the banks of the Columbia gathered each day to watch the party run the rapids. To their amazement, the explorers made it through unharmed.

They sighted the Pacific on November 7, 1805. Clark's journal entry captures their immense relief: "Ocian in view. O! the joy." To celebrate, Lewis and Clark carved their names in a tree near the mouth of the Columbia and added, "By land from the U. States in 1804 & 1805." Clark estimated that they had traveled more than 4,100 miles (6,598 km) from their starting point in Illinois. After two years of hardship and adventure, they had reached their goal.

After two years, the expedition finally reached the Pacific Ocean.

Fort Clatsop.

Tuesday January 1st 1806.

Clatsop Paddle 5 feet long
4 In. greatest width of blade.

Quath-lah-poh-tle Smoard
3 feet in length. some of
them are near 4 feet in length.
and 4½ inches in width at the
widest part. —

form of the wooden
bludgeon used by the
same people. —

This photograph shows a page from Lewis's journal during the time the expedition spent at Fort Clatsop.

Chapter Five

The Trip Home

Before the expedition could return home, they had to survive another grueling winter in the West. They spent those winter months in a damp wooden fort they built near present-day Astoria, Oregon. That winter was as damp and chilly as their previous winter had been bitter cold. Between November 4 and March 25, they had only twelve days without rain. Just keeping the fire going was hard work because the firewood was so damp in Fort Clatsop. The men were bored and restless. To keep them busy, Lewis and Clark set up a salt-making camp near the ocean. Taking turns in groups of three, the men

A Historic Vote

At the Pacific, Lewis and Clark had to pick a spot to spend the winter. They considered moving back up the Columbia River, where game would be more plentiful. If they stayed near the coast, though, there was a small chance they'd spot an American or British trading ship. To settle their **dilemma**, the commanders let the party decide by voting. Sacagawea voted and so did York.

It was a historic event. It was the first time in American history a black slave had voted. It was also the first time a woman had voted. The decision was to look for a campsite on the south bank of the Columbia, not far from the coast. By December 7, they started building Fort Clatsop, near present-day Astoria, Oregon. The group moved in on Christmas Eve, 1805.

boiled down salty seawater and scraped the sides of the large kettles to obtain salt. They used the salt to preserve the meat the hunters brought in.

Mapping the West

Clark worked on a map of the country they had covered over the last two years. Lewis made notes of the plants, trees, and animals he had observed. He described or preserved ten new plants and trees, including the beautiful Sitka spruce. He also wrote about eleven birds, eleven mammals, and two fish then unknown to naturalists. He described the wolverine and the

A sketch of the California condor from the Lewis and Clark's journals

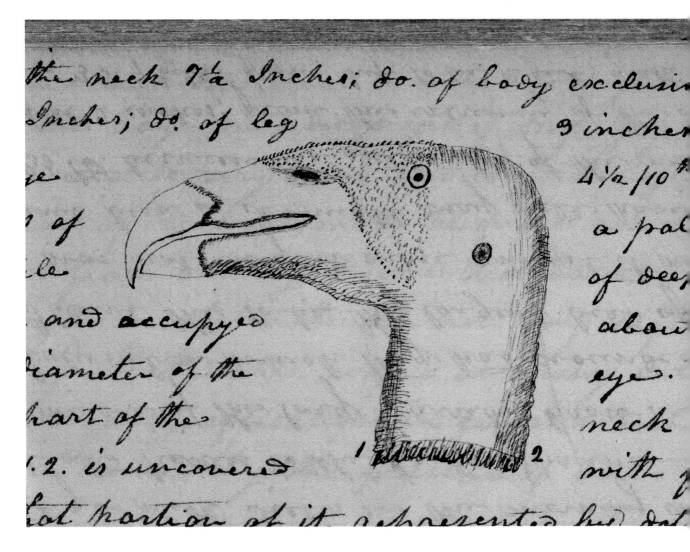

California condor, the largest bird in North America, and made sketches of gulls, vultures, and trout.

These notes and maps fulfilled many of the objectives Jefferson had outlined at the start of their journey. They were among the expedition's most important achievements. But unless they made it back home safely, the world would never know of them.

Eager to make that return trip, the expedition headed back up the Columbia River on March 23. By May, they were back in Nez Percé country, where they stayed for six weeks with their old friends. They waited there for the snow in the mountains to melt. After several attempts, they finally made it across the mountains. Safely out of the Bitterroots, Lewis and Clark decided to split their party. Lewis took a small group north to explore the Marias River. Clark headed south with most of the party to explore the Yellowstone River. Lewis had the more difficult task. He would be traveling through the lands of the hostile Blackfeet Indians. On July 26, his party encountered a group of Blackfeet and they settled down to camp for the night with the Indians. They woke the next morning to find the Indians trying to steal their guns and horses. In the gunfight that followed, Lewis's men killed two Blackfeet. The explorers escaped unharmed to the Missouri River.

The expedition returned to the Mandan villages in mid-August. Soon they were making 70 to 80 miles (113 to 129 km) each day, with the river's current in their favor. Now, almost daily, they met traders heading upstream. Already, the

A member of the expedition fires at the Blackfeet.

Making Maps

Clark was the main mapmaker for the Corps of Discovery. He and Lewis had the best navigational tools at their disposal. But most of all, they used dead reckoning to figure out how far they'd traveled—guessing the distance from one fixed point to another. For short distances, they used a two-pole chain—a 33-foot (10-m) chain stretched between two sticks. This was how Lewis and Clark mapped an entire continent. Before their trip, most maps of the West showed a single ridge of mountains that could be easily crossed. Clark's maps showed a whole series of mountain chains that would make travel difficult. They also showed that the continent was much wider than anyone had imagined.

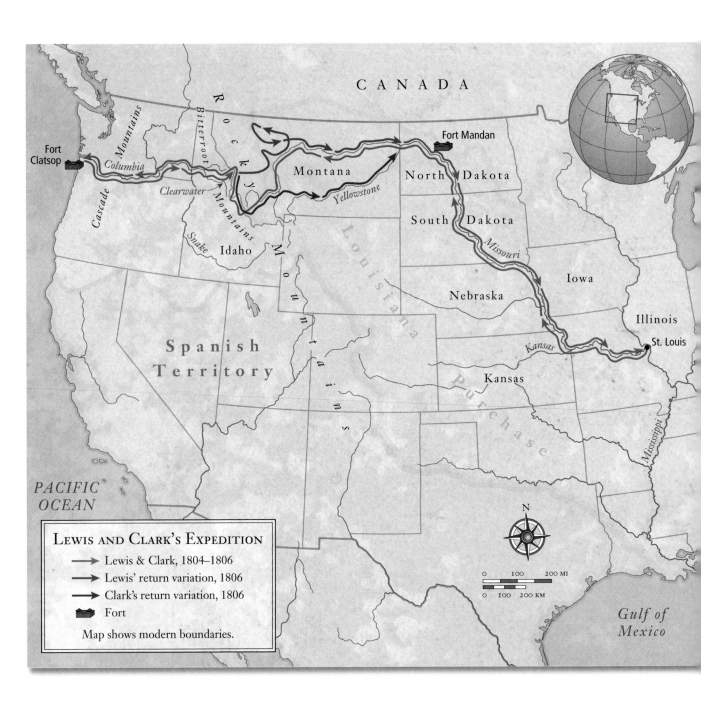

CANADA

Fort Mandan

Fort Clatsop

PACIFIC OCEAN

Gulf of Mexico

Rocky Mountains

Bitterroot Mountains

Cascade Mountains

Columbia

Clearwater

Snake

Yellowstone

Missouri

Kansas

Mississippi

Montana

North Dakota

South Dakota

Nebraska

Iowa

Illinois

St. Louis

Kansas

Idaho

Spanish Territory

Louisiana Purchase

N

LEWIS AND CLARK'S EXPEDITION

→ Lewis & Clark, 1804–1806

→ Lewis' return variation, 1806

→ Clark's return variation, 1806

▬ Fort

Map shows modern boundaries.

0   100   200 MI

0   100   200 KM

lower stretches of the Missouri were becoming well traveled. As they passed the frontier villages near the mouth of the Missouri, the explorers must have paddled extra hard. Every stroke was bringing them closer to the end of their great journey. On September 23, the members of the Corps of Discovery glided into St. Louis amid great fanfare. They had been given up for lost by many. But after two years, their journey was over.

During their trip home, Lewis and Clark saw many people building homes near the river's mouth.

Lewis and Clark returned home to tell the rest of the country of the beauty and wonders of the West.

Chapter Six

In Their Footsteps

Lewis and Clark were now national heroes. But they still had a lot of work to do. One of the first things Lewis did was write a long letter to Jefferson. He had plenty of good news for the President: The explorers were home safely, the West was rich in resources, and the rivers were full of beavers and otters—animals whose fur **pelts** were very valuable. There was bad news though. There was no easy water route through the mountains to the Pacific Ocean.

After the expedition, William Clark spent the rest of his career as a government official in the West.

Still, Jefferson wanted Lewis to publish his official report on the expedition. But Lewis never finished his report. Not long after his return, he became governor of the Louisiana Territory. The many duties of his new job proved to be too much for Lewis. He fell into deep debt. He began to express his despair to Clark and other friends. Finally, in 1809, he headed for Washington to clear up a financial dispute. On October 11, 1809, near Nashville, Tennessee, he took his own life.

Like Lewis, Clark took an important government job in St. Louis. He was named superintendent of Indian affairs for the Louisiana Territory. In 1813, he became governor of the newly formed Missouri Territory. In both jobs, he worked to protect Indians during the westward expansion of the United States. He married Julia "Judith" Hancock—the woman for whom he'd named a river in the West. They named their first son Meriwether Lewis Clark—after Clark's partner in exploration. Clark died at age 69 on September 1, 1838.

The Legacies of Lewis and Clark

Before Lewis and Clark's journey, the map of the western part of the North American continent was largely blank. They filled it in. The landscape of the American West was a mystery. They described it. The animal and plant life of the land beyond the Rockies was the subject of speculation. They carefully cataloged it.

Lewis and Clark gave the United States its first glimpse of the immensity and variety of the American West. They

Through their travels, Lewis and Clark made many discoveries about the people, places, and animals found in the West.

described 178 plants and 122 animal species and subspecies never before cataloged. They recorded the traditions, manners, and languages of 40 American Indian tribes. And not only their two leaders, but seven of their men as well, kept valuable journals of their trip.

They were the first U.S. citizens to see the Rocky Mountains. They were the first to cross the continent. They were the first to reach the Pacific Ocean by land. Their explorations strengthened U.S. claims to the Pacific Northwest and spurred westward expansion. Lewis and Clark provided a model of enlightened exploration for the future. They established good relations with most of the Indian tribes they met. And their journey added immensely to the world's store of knowledge.

They discovered that there was no quick water route to the Pacific, but in their footsteps came trappers, traders, adventurers, and settlers. They opened the American West to the people of the United States.

Many people decided to move to the American West after Lewis and Clark's expedition.

Timeline

1770	William Clark is born in Caroline County in Virginia on August 1.
1774	Meriwether Lewis is born in Albermarle County in Virginia on August 18.
1801	Thomas Jefferson asks Lewis to serve as his personal secretary on March 6.
1803	Lewis agrees to lead exploration of West and asks Clark to share command with him.
1803	United States purchases Louisiana Territory from France on July 4.
1804	Corps of Discovery begins trip up Missouri River on May 14.
1804	Sergeant Charles Floyd dies on August 20.
1804	Trapper Charbonneau signs on with expedition and brings his pregnant wife Sacagawea.
1805	Jean Baptiste Charbonneau is born on February 13.
1805	Lewis and Clark reach Pacific Ocean in November.
1806	Lewis's party encounter Blackfeet on July 26–27.
1806	Lewis and Clark return to St. Louis on September 23.
1809	Lewis takes his own life near Nashville, Tennessee, on October 11.
1838	William Clark dies in St. Louis on September 1.

Glossary

bluff—a steep hill or cliff

botany—the study of plants

casualty—a person who is killed or injured

compass—an instrument for determining directions, with a magnetic needle that always points north

dilemma—a difficult choice

fauna—the animals of a certain region

flora—the plants of a certain region

game—wild animals hunted for food or sport

grueling—very tiring or exhausting

Indian country—a term used for parts of the western United States occupied by American Indians

keelboat—a shallow-bottomed boat, used on rivers

militia—a military group made up of ordinary people

naturalist—someone who specializes in natural history and studies plants, animals, and their environments

pelt—the fur and skin of an animal

pirogue—a large, flat-bottomed rowboat

pneumonia—a type of lung disease

portage—carrying boats and other goods overland from one waterway to another

prickly pear—a kind of cactus plant with pear-shaped fruit

ravine—a deep, narrow valley

secretary—someone who handles letters and other papers

swath—a path cut in a long strip

woolly mammoth—an extinct species of elephant

To Find Out More

Books

Jones, Veda Boyd. *Thomas Jefferson: Author of the Declaration of Independence*. Philadelphia: Chelsea House, 2000.

Morley, Jacqueline. *Across America: The Story of Lewis and Clark*. Danbury, CT: Franklin Watts, 1998.

Stefoff, Rebecca. *Lewis and Clark: Explorers of the American West*. Philadelphia: Chelsea House, 1992.

Thorp, Daniel B. *Lewis and Clark: An American Journey*. New York: Metro Books, 1998.

White Alana J. *Sacagawea: Westward with Lewis and Clark*. Springfield, NJ: Enslow, 1997.

Organizations and Online Sites

Discovering Lewis and Clark
http://www.lewis-clark.org/index.htm
Learn more about Lewis and Clark's expedition, from biographies of the Corps of the Discovery to information about the people, animals, and plants found along the way. This site also provides excerpts from Lewis and Clark's journals.

Fort Clatsop National Memorial
http://www.nps.gov/focl/
Discover Fort Clatsop—Lewis and Clark's winter camp—now a national memorial.

Lewis and Clark Bicentennial Council
Lewis & Clark College
0615 SW Palatine Hill Road
Portland, OR 97219
http://www.lewisandclark200.org/
This organization is dedicated to honoring the bicentennial of Lewis and Clark's expedition.

Lewis and Clark: The Journey of the Corps of Discovery
http://www.pbs.org/lewisandclark
Created as a companion to Ken Burns' documentary, this online site provides a wealth of information about the expedition.

Lewis and Clark in North Dakota
http://www.ndlewisandclark.com/
This online site offers profiles of Lewis and Clark and some of the American Indian leaders they encountered on their expedition, maps, as well as interesting trivia about the expedition.

Lewis and Clark Trail
http://www.nps.gov/lecl/welcome.htm
Learn more about the Lewis and Clark Trail from the National Park Service. This online site features the history of the trail and information on sites along the trail.

Videos

Biography: Lewis and Clark, Explorers of the New Frontier. A&E Biography, 1999.

Lewis and Clark: The Journey of the Corps of Discovery. PBS Home Video, 1997.

A Note on Sources

One historian called Lewis and Clark "the writingest explorers." Both Lewis and Clark kept journals on their expedition, as did several of their men. Their journals are still the best way to get to know Lewis and Clark and to appreciate their accomplishments.

I also consulted a number of outstanding histories and biographies, including *The Way to the Western Sea* by David Lavender, *Lewis and Clark* by Ron Appleman, and *Undaunted Courage* by Stephen E. Ambrose. Daniel B. Botkin's *Our Natural History* provided much insight into the natural world the explorers encountered. At Chicago's Newberry Library, I found E. G. Chuinard's *Only One Man Died*, which offered information on the medical aspects of the expedition.

At every stage of my research, I depended on the expertise of librarians. I wish to thank them for their help.

—*Andrew Santella*

Index

Numbers in *italics* indicate illustrations.

About the Author

Andrew Santella writes from Chicago. He is the author of several books for young people, most of them on the history of the United States. He also writes about sports, books, and many other topics for publications like *GQ* and *The New York Times Book Review*. He is a graduate of Loyola University in Chicago.